BELLA

The Little Furry Chiweenie Who Saved Our Lives

Michael J. Whelan

BELLA

Copyright © 2025 by Michael J. Whelan

All rights reserved.

No part of this book may be reproduced or transmitted in any form or by an electronic or mechanical means, including photocopying, recording or by any information storage and retrieval system, without the express written permission of the publisher, except where permitted by law.

Published by Michael J. Whelan
Edited by Maryann Miller
Cover Design and Formatting by The Book Khaleesi
Cover Image: Original Painting by Rebecca Whelan
Illustrated by Michael J. Whelan

TABLE OF CONTENTS

ACKNOWLEDGEMENTS	5
DEDICATION	7
CHAPTER ONE	
The Day I'll Never Forget	1
CHAPTER TWO	
Rebecca, Revelation, and the Greenie Gambit	11
CHAPTER THREE	
Lessons From a Dog Who Knows Things	19
CHAPTER FOUR	
Queen Bella, Emotional Support and Treat Negotiator	25
CHAPTER FIVE	
The Talk I Didn't Know I Needed	33
CHAPTER SIX	
The Best Day in a Long Time	41
CHAPTER SEVEN	
The Spotlight Finds Bella	49
CHAPTER EIGHT	
What Bella Gave Rebecca	56
CHAPTER NINE	
Lavender and Light	60
CHAPTER TEN	
Honoring Bella's Request	64
POSTSCRIPT: FROM BELLA	
(With Love and Peanut Butter Breath)	71

ACKNOWLEDGEMENTS

To my dear friend, Maryann Miller—

Thank you for stepping in with such heart and brilliance to help shape the final touches of Bella. You didn't just polish the pages—you lifted the spirit of the story, honoring every beat of its quirky, snarky, tender heart. This picture book for grown-ups is about hope, healing, and the power of laughter through tears—and your friendship gave those themes even more light.

Your generosity, guidance, and unwavering belief in this project (and in me) were nothing short of lifesaving. You brought clarity when I was lost in the fog of edits, and kindness when I was teetering on the edge of self-doubt. Bella is better because of you.

And to my wife, Rebecca, my partner for life—

You've always been my muse. My steady flame in the dark. Thank you for inspiring me, loving me, and—forgive me—tolerating the clatter of my keyboard during countless sleepless nights. You've given me more grace than I deserve and more courage than I thought I had. Without you, I wouldn't be the man I am. I wouldn't be the artist I am. And I certainly wouldn't be writing stories like this.
This book carries both your fingerprints—
Maryann's on the page, Rebecca's on my heart.

With all my love and deepest gratitude,

Michael

DEDICATION

To the quiet warriors and the loud-hearted fighters—

This book is for all those who have faced cancer or Parkinson's, or both, and somehow found the strength to keep moving forward. For the ones whose hands tremble, whose bodies ache, whose spirits have been tested beyond imagination—and still, you rise.

It's for the caregivers, too. The ones who stay when others leave. Who memorize medication charts, hold back tears, and whisper encouragement through sleepless nights. You carry the weight of two souls.

And, as Bella would say, you are the heartbeat behind the healing.

CHAPTER ONE

The Day I'll Never Forget

I used to think miracles were rare—reserved for saints, lottery winners, and people who make it through the TSA line without losing their dignity.

Then one day my dog, Bella started talking. Yep! You heard that correctly.

But, I'm getting a little bit ahead of myself.

Here's the setup: I'm seventy years old. A three-time cancer survivor and the caregiver to my wife Rebecca who has Parkinson's.

And on this particular day in August, I was driving my 2011 Nissan Juke to the hospital for my very last chemotherapy treatment.

That car? My Juke. It rattled like a tambourine in a hurricane and my A/C only works once I have arrived at my destination.

BELLA

But it still ran. And so did this old guy.
And riding shotgun, as always, was my Bella.
My rescue Chiweenie.
Part dog.
Part therapist.
But all heart.
She sat upright without a leash, her head high, ears alert, eyes focused like a general surveying a battlefield.
Her confidence always amazed me.
She also happened to shed like a dandelion caught in a leaf blower.
Her fur floated through the Juke like glitter at a parade.
I'd long since given up on fighting it.
Her hair was part of the upholstery now—just like she was a part of our lives.
Today, I was dressed like a man who'd either lost a bet or knew exactly what he was doing—bright pink sneakers the color of Pepto Bismol, a flamingo-pink Hawaiian shirt, black pants, and socks.
One sock was decorated with cats - the other covered by dogs.
And of course, atop my head sat my favorite pink baseball cap with big white block letters that screamed:
NEVER EVER GIVE UP
When you have cancer, and your body's at war with itself, and your spirit's running on fumes, sometimes the only thing you can do is wear something louder than your fear.
Whenever I caught my reflection in the hospital's glass doors, it made me smile.
And some days, that smile was the only thing that got me inside the hospital and through the day.

But before we went in, Bella leaned over and gently licked my hand. It was her way of saying, 'we've got this, cowboy. Now let's go get em'!

And at that very moment it brought me back to a different time…

A time almost eleven years ago, when my wife Rebecca and I walked into a rescue shelter in Orlando.

Just to look around.

We weren't planning on adopting a pet.

Hell, I could barely take care of myself, let alone add a dog to the mix.

Still, I felt a pull. Something seemed to say, "Why not?"

The volunteer at the center asked if we wanted to see the "easy" dogs.

I shook my head. "Nope. Show me the ones nobody wants."

So, they took us to the back of the building, an area that I didn't even know existed.

And that's where we found her—curled in the corner of a crate, silent and small, like she was trying to vanish into the wall.

"She used to be a service dog," the volunteer said. "Her owner died suddenly.

She was with him when it happened. Since then… she hasn't connected with anyone."

"No name. No tags. We just call her 'the little one'."

Rebecca knelt down—her hand soft and slow like it always is—and she reached through the bars.

The little dog didn't flinch. Didn't bark.

She cautiously leaned into Rebecca's palm and exhaled the saddest sigh I'd ever heard.

The volunteer repeated, "She doesn't really connect well with people."

BELLA

"That's perfect," I said. "Neither do I." My response catching the volunteer completely off guard.

That afternoon we brought the little dog home. And somehow, she brought us home, as well.

Later that evening, after we had crawled into bed, she curled up carefully at the foot near Rebecca's legs.

She, The Little One, was so quiet.

Watchful. Shivering. Like she wasn't sure if she was allowed to stay.

Rebecca ran her hand along the dog's back and whispered, "Her name's going to be Bella. Because she's so beautiful."

It was the first word that felt right. So Bella it was.

She didn't wag her tail. She didn't bark.

She just closed her eyes and let out another sigh—this time, like someone who finally felt safe.

And somehow, she never left that moment.

Now, eleven years later, parked outside the cancer hospital, her head resting on my leg - the world trembling around us—she still carried that same quiet loyalty.

That silent promise: I'm here. Always.

We walked through those automatic glass doors like veterans of a war that the two of us had never signed up for.

The nurses spotted us, and immediately smiles lit up their faces.

"There he is!" One nurse called out. "Our Rainbow Warrior!"

I flexed my muscles just to add a bit of humor, did a little breakdance and tipped my cap. "Boys and girls it's always a pleasure to perform here at the hospital. Any donation of any kind is certainly welcomed."

Chuckles all around, then another nurse called out as I came close, "If oncology ever hosts a fashion show, you're headlining it, Michael."

I laughed. "The colors are for me," I told her. "When I catch my reflection, even I have to smile.

"And if I can smile, then maybe I can show up and that's half the battle in the world of cancer."

"You couldn't be more right. Keep showing up," she said, patting my arm. "You make people braver. You give them hope. You make a difference."

I was overwhelmed by their words. "Then the colors are well worth it." I replied.

Bella gave a low, approving grunt wagging her tail at warp speed as she rolled in circles on the floor.

"By the way, she's my stylist," I said pointing at the furry tornado.

"And my emotional backup system as well, when bribing the staff with actual currency fails."

We made our way to the infusion room. Same hallway. Same room. Same recliner. Same spot.

The chair groaned beneath me, like it remembered every bruise, every hour I'd spent in it.

Bella curled up at my feet, her usual cinnamon-roll spiral of devotion.

And then out of the blue…

She spoke.

"Well," Bella said, stretching her legs delicately, "this place still smells like sadness and weak coffee—but the graham crackers—are top-notch, so I'll approve this unfortunate mishap one more time."

I blinked and shook my head.

I stared at her.

BELLA

Then at my IV line.
At the nurses walking by.
And then back at her.
"Bella?"
She looked up. "Yes? Okay, I know, it might be a bit of a shock but I'm still adorable. But now I come with bonus dialogue. It doesn't get much better than that."
"You?... you can talk?"
"I've always been able to talk. You just weren't listening.
"Or, maybe I wasn't ready for you to hear me.
"Timing's everything, Michael. Ask any great artist."
My mouth dried up. "Why now?"
Her eyes grew thoughtful.
"Because it's your last chemo treatment. Surprise!"
Bella paused for a moment looking pensive.
"And sometimes the ones we love need to hear the words we've been saving—before we run out of time."
My throat tightened. My chest ached.
She rested her chin on her paws. "I've spent years lying under these chairs. Watching. Listening. Hoping."
"Hoping for what?" I whispered.
"That everyone in this room had someone like you do.
"Someone to hold their hand.
"Someone to drive them home.
"To sit with them in the silence.
"To love them to pieces.
"Not everyone has that, and THAT breaks my heart."
"Bella..." I wiped my eyes. It didn't stop the tears.
"You and Rebecca saved me," she said. "I just wanted to give something back to everyone. I'm not just here for you.
"I'm here for everyone going through this horrible disease."

MICHAEL J. WHELAN

I stared at Bella.

She added, "This morning, when you looked in the mirror, your hat said Never Ever Give Up, but your eyes. They didn't look as convinced and that worried me."

I touched the brim of my hat. "I'm still here, Bella."

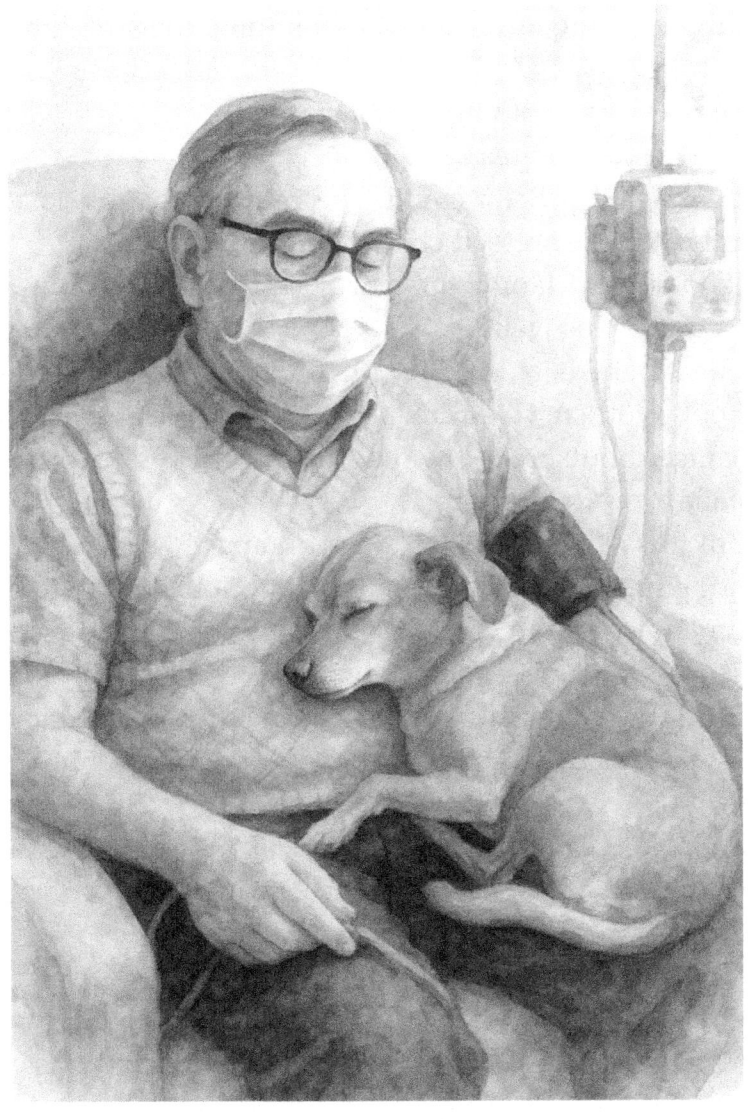

BELLA

She climbed gently into my lap, placed one paw over my heart, and then drooled all over my brand-new shirt.

"I know you are, Michael. And so am I.

"For every needle. Every scan.

"Every cry you tried to muffle in the shower so Rebecca didn't hear you—I heard it all and it broke my little heart.

"I'm not going anywhere." I attempted to assure her. And then I broke.

She let me cry into her fur. My mouth was covered in her hair but it didn't matter.

Then, as only Bella could, she muttered, "You taste like salt, coffee, and repressed childhood trauma."

I let out a half-laugh, half-sob. "This is insane. Now you're doing stand-up as well?"

Bella laughed.

"Look, you survived hospital grilled cheese sandwiches, three cancer bouts, and a wife who thinks cookies, cakes and jellybeans are a food group.

"But this is the thing that rips you apart?"

She sighed. "Humans. You're so emotionally constipated."

A man across the room, looked over, and Bella leaned in to whisper, "Michael, I just wanted to let you know. If that guy nods off, I'm stealing his peanut butter crackers. He has more than he needs and he chews like a wood chipper in a wind tunnel."

"Bella! You can't say things like that!"

"I'm just saying what everyone else in here is too polite to say."

A nurse passed by.

Bella sniffed the air.

"And by the way—she's wearing a perfume that's called

MICHAEL J. WHELAN

Date Night: Canceled by Text. That's why she looks sad today."

"Bella!" I couldn't help but shake my head.

"I'm not here to be polite. I'm here to be honest."

The rest of the time in treatment passed by rather quickly, made easier with a dog in my lap talking to me.

And then came the nurse with the clipboard.

"You're all done, Michael. Are you ready to ring the bell?"

Bella stood, her tail wagging gently.

"I've got an idea, let's do it together," she said.

"Great idea!" I said.

So, I lifted her little body into my arms, walked to the bell, and placed my hand over her tiny paws.

BELLA

We rang that big old bell three times with intention.
Like we really meant it!
It was Loud. It was Clear.
And hopefully, it was Final.
The nurses and other patients clapped.
I wept.
Bella leaned in close and whispered, "Make sure you remember this sound—forever.
"For the quiet days. The lonely ones.
"When you need to remember what it feels like to win."
She didn't say another word.
She just stayed pressed against my chest and let me cry.
This wasn't just the end of chemo.
And when your dog starts talking—really talking—it's not the end of your sanity.
It's all the beginning of your arc of redemption which includes:
A comedy.
A comeback.
A graham-cracker-fueled miracle.
The renewing of everything I thought I'd lost:
Laughter.
Love.
Magic.
Hope.
And I wasn't facing it alone.
Not with Bella riding shotgun.
And for one sacred, ridiculous, magnificent moment—it was just my little service dog and me.
One stitched back together by science.
The other sent by something much holier.

CHAPTER TWO

Rebecca, Revelation, and the Greenie Gambit

After leaving the hospital, I drove home with Bella next to me in the passenger seat.

The drive felt oddly peaceful.

Even after everything that had happened—chemo, the bell, and the fact that my dog had just spoken to me in front of a room full of strangers—there was this serenity inside the car.

Almost like a new chapter had started, and we were just figuring out how to turn the page.

I glanced over at her, still wondering if I had imagined it.

Maybe the whole thing was some kind of strange dream.

But no. She was right there, awake, alert, and now eyeing the world out the window like she always did.

I couldn't shake the feeling that something big had shifted, and we hadn't quite grasped what it all meant yet.

BELLA

I parked the car in the garage, still trying to absorb the weight of what had just happened.

We walked into the house, and I saw Rebecca sitting in her favorite chair, a plush blue blanket tucked around her legs.

She was watching QVC, the room filled with the gentle light of the afternoon sun, but the second she saw us, it was like she could tell something was different.

She looked at Bella, then back at me, her brow furrowing.

Bella did what she always did when we returned home; she spun in circles in front of Rebecca until she exhausted herself—then she just had to lie down.

"You two are home early. How was it?"

I took a deep breath, and then looked down at Bella, still at my feet ready for her nap, her tail swishing in that lazy way of hers.

The way she was when she knew something important was about to happen.

"Well, we—" I gestured to Bella, "—we have something to tell you."

Rebecca squinted at me, confused, and then looked at Bella again. "What do you mean?"

"I mean," I said slowly, still unsure if I even believed it myself, "Bella can talk now."

Rebecca's expression went from confusion, to disbelief, and then to complete shock.

She laughed nervously, glancing between me and Bella. "Michael, you've got to be kidding. What are you—"

"Not a joke," I said, "I'm serious. She spoke to me today, in the hospital, while we were waiting for the chemo to finish."

"Just… casually spoke."

Rebecca's eyes widened. She looked at Bella, then back at

me, as if I'd just suggested that a whale had just walked through our living room and decided to move into our guest room.

"You... you're telling me Bella—my Bella—our Bella—spoke to you? Like you and I are talking right now?"

"Yep.

"Except with a lot less fur flying around the room.

"She told me I looked like I was about to quit and give up. She said, my eyes gave it away."

Rebecca blinked. "She... told you that?"

"Yes," I said, finally convinced that I wasn't losing my mind.

"She said she knew when I was ready to quit, and she didn't want that to happen. After everything we've been through. She's sticking with me and you."

Rebecca let out a soft laugh, but it was shaky and uncertain.

She shook her head, her face a mix of amusement and disbelief.

"I mean, that's insane. Just... completely insane." Then her expression softened. "But if Bella's gonna pick the moment to talk, I guess this is as good a time as any."

I watched Rebecca carefully, waiting for the skepticism to completely fade.

And it did, slowly, as she focused intently on Bella's happy expression. looked at Bella, then back at me.

"But, Michael... why now?"

"Why would she wait all this time?"

I took a seat in the chair beside Rebecca, and Bella followed to curl at my feet again. Now clearly aware that her two humans were in full-blown processing mode.

BELLA

"I think…" I paused, trying to make sense of it myself. "I think she was just waiting for me to be ready.

"For us to be ready.

"You know, we've been through so much these last eleven years.

"Between my cancer. Your Parkinson's. Everything in between. Maybe we just needed a moment where we could hear each other."

Rebecca's face filled with love as she reached down and gently stroked Bella's soft furry head. "I always knew you had wisdom in those little eyes of yours," she whispered to Bella, her voice full of affection and wonder.

Bella's tail wagged lazily, but there was something in the way she looked up at Rebecca that said it all.

"My gosh. Well, that explains the side-eye she's been giving me every time I wear my sweater covered with images of cats.

"Honestly, if she starts offering life advice and emotional support in full sentences, I might just retire from house work and let her take over.

"But I swear, if she tells me I'm hogging the bed, I'm out."

We both laughed. A laugh we've kept buried for a long time.

She wasn't just a dog anymore.

She was part of this family, the unsung hero we never realized we needed.

"So, you're telling me," Rebecca said, leaning forward, still processing, "that Bella has been able to talk. The whole time she's been here?"

"Yeah," I said, laughing softly. "She's been under our noses this whole time, saving her best material for the right moment."

BELLA

Rebecca gave me a playful side-eye, then reached down and gently lifted Bella onto her lap, cradling her like a baby. "I don't even know where to start.

"You're saying that this little dog has been listening to me cry, watching us go through everything, and only now she's going to chime in with her opinion?"

I chuckled. "Well, she's got a lot of opinions. And she's not afraid to share them. Be careful what you wish for."

Bella yawned, and then turned her head slightly to look at Rebecca, tail wagging, as if to say, "This is me, and I'm here for you, too."

Rebecca's eyes dimmed and she looked down at Bella, the realization settling in that this wasn't some cute trick or moment of whimsy. This was something more. "I'm glad she's here," Rebecca said lovingly, her voice full of emotion. "I really am.

And if anyone is going to make sure you don't lose your mind, it's her."

Bella, lifted her head to lick Rebecca's cheek, a perfect display of affection, before her eyes shifted to me with that familiar, wise look.

And then she said, in that voice I'd never heard before today.

"Are you two done? Enough of this Hallmark Card moment guys, I think we should go to PetSmart."

Rebecca blinked as she almost fell off out of her chair. "What the...?"

"Michael just spent thirty minutes telling you that I can talk.

"I've come to the conclusion that I deserve one of those dental Greenies and some of those puppy ice creams," Bella said matter-of-factly.

"And while we're at it, I think we should console that little boy who's there every time we go in. He breaks my heart.

"You know. The one who always looks so sad."

"Max," I said, suddenly remembering the young boy we'd seen several times in the waiting room where pets for adoption were housed in cages.

Max had told us about a month ago that his dog, Chester, had recently died, and he liked to come to the pet store to watch the kittens and puppies play.

In all the times we'd seen him at the store, the sadness had never left his eyes.

Bella nodded, her tail swishing like she knew what was coming next. "Yes. Max. He could use some Bella-love today. Let's go cheer him up."

Rebecca and I exchanged a look, and shrugged.

Somehow, despite everything, the overwhelming absurdity of it all… it felt right.

I drove us to PetSmart later that afternoon, Bella sitting proudly in the backseat, as if the whole world was her personal playground.

When we walked in, I noticed Max sitting by the dog toy aisle, his face still marked with that quiet sadness. When he looked up and saw Bella, his eyes lit up.

Bella trotted over, tail wagging furiously, and sat down in front of him, offering her most comforting look. "Hi there, Max," she said softly. "I know you're missing your dog. But you're not alone. Not when there's a dog like me around."

Max's face broke into the smallest smile, as though he'd never imagined that a dog might want to talk to him, let alone give him this kind of comfort.

He reached down to pet Bella, and for the first time since

BELLA

we'd met him, the tension in his face relaxed.

I could hear Bella whisper, "It gets better, Max. Not all at once, but it does. I promise you that"

I turned to Rebecca, who had tears in her eyes, and said, "I can't believe what we're seeing. She's incredible."

Rebecca smiled softly, wiping her eyes. "She always has been."

CHAPTER THREE

Lessons From a Dog Who Knows Things

That night, I couldn't sleep.

My body was exhausted, but my mind was on fire—overthinking everything from whether the cancer was truly gone, to how in the hell I was supposed to live a normal life now that my dog had started talking.

Bella lay curled beside me, her back pressed against mine, breathing slow and steady. I could feel the warmth from her little body heating the entire bed. She always knew when I needed her close. Like some kind of living barometer for emotional storms.

"You're staring at the ceiling again," she said without even opening her eyes.

"Yes, I just noticed that it needs painting. Besides I thought you were asleep," I murmured.

"I was. Then your soul started pacing. Michael, do humans ever chase squirrels in their sleep?"

BELLA

I chuckled. "No! And I'm sorry for keeping your soul up."

"It's okay," she whispered, "We've both got a lot to carry."

There was silence for a while. Not uncomfortable—just the kind that exists between two beings who understand each other so deeply that they don't always need words.

But tonight … I needed words.

"Do you ever get scared, Bella?" I asked quietly. "I mean, really scared!"

Bella shifted just enough to rest her chin on my shoulder—while she pondered the question. "All the time, Michael."

I turned slightly. "Even when you're with me?"

"Especially when I'm with you," she said. "Because I love you so much.

"And love makes us brave, but it also makes us vulnerable. I'm scared of losing you and Rebecca."

That one landed. Deep in my soul.

"I understand." I looked at her, at those impossibly wise eyes.

"You saved me, you know. I don't mean just today.

"I mean years ago.

"That day we found you in the shelter.

"You were the first one who didn't ask me to pretend I was okay."

Bella didn't respond at first. She just let the silence breathe. Then she said, "You saved me too. I didn't even have a name.

"Didn't want one.

"I was just waiting for something to end.

"But then you and Rebecca walked in, and I thought… maybe this is the beginning instead."

Tears stung the corners of my eyes.

Again.

I was getting soft in my old age.

Or maybe just real.

I rolled onto my side, and Bella, always intuitive, scooted closer.

She tucked her tiny head under my chin like a warm river stone.

"I don't want to die," I whispered.

"I know you don't," she said. "None of us do!"

"But if I do, I want to make sure Rebecca's okay. And that you're okay."

"I'll take care of her," Bella said simply. "She took care of me.

"That's how life works. We all pay it forward."

"I can't imagine not being here."

Bella sighed. "You don't have to imagine it tonight. Tonight, you're here. You're breathing. You're wrapped in sheets that smell like fabric softener and dog dander.

"And you've got me.

"Tomorrow will come when it comes."

She paused, then added, "And when it does, I'll be right here.

"Probably asking me to fetch you an ice cream cup from the freezer." I laughed through the lump in my throat.

Bella stretched, hopped off the bed with a grunt, and padded into the kitchen.

"What are you doing?" I called.

"You said 'ice cream.' You think I'm not going to act on that?"

I shook my head, slipped out of bed, and followed her down the hall.

The house was quiet, humming with the refrigerator's rhythm and the occasional creak of its old bones.

BELLA

I grabbed one of the little vanilla puppy cups we kept stashed behind the frozen peas and handed it to her.

She took it delicately between her teeth, and then placed it on the floor, looking up at me. "You first," she said.

"What?"

"Sit," she ordered. "It's your turn. I've been your therapist, spiritual guide, nurse, and snack scout. But now? You need to talk. Really talk."

So I sat on the floor, back against the cabinets. Bella settled down beside me.

"I'm tired," I said.

"I know," she replied. "I can see it every day."

"Not just chemo-tired. Soul-tired. World-tired." I struggled to get the words out.

Bella rested her paw on my knee.

"You've been carrying too much for too long," she said. "You take care of Rebecca. All of us.

"You worry about money. I see you staring at those stacks of bills…

"You write stories for people. Hoping someone will read them. Hoping it will all matter before the clock runs out.

"And you never let anyone see how much it costs you. I find that all inspiring."

I didn't respond.

I couldn't.

Then she whispered the one thing that broke me: "It's okay to need help, Michael."

The tears came fast. Not loud. Just real. I sat on the floor with my tiny miracle of a dog and let myself fall apart. I'd cried more in the past two days than I had the entire year.

She didn't lick my face this time. She didn't joke. She just leaned into me and stayed.

And after a while, when the tears dried and the silence settled in again, she looked up and said, "A big ol' belly rub wouldn't hurt right about now."

BELLA

I laughed. "That's more like it."

And I scratched her belly until her leg kicked like a jackhammer and she sighed like a queen being fanned with palm fronds.

"You know what you are?" I said as I stood to head back to bed.

"Stunning. Radiant. Emotionally mature?"

I smiled. "You're my guardian angel, Bella."

She paused in the doorway, her tail wagging slowly.

"No wings," she said, "but I make it work."

CHAPTER FOUR

Queen Bella, Emotional Support and Treat Negotiator

The next morning started the way most days do around here, with fur in my mouth and my eyes glued together from Bella's dander.

"Ugh," I groaned, spitting out what could only be described as a hairball. "Bella, were you trying to suffocate me in my sleep?"

She was already standing proudly on my chest like a furry sphinx, tail wagging and eyes wide.

"Technically, it was a cuddle. But if you go, I get your sock drawer, so it's a win-win."

I laughed, even as I reached for the water glass on my nightstand.

Rebecca stirred beside me. "Is she up talking again?" she murmured, still groggy.

BELLA

"Nonstop," I said. "She's basically a motivational speaker now—with a criminal record – theft of ice cream and snacks."

Bella bowed theatrically. "Guilty. But adorable.

"Now—belly rub or I'll lick your nose until it glows like Rudolf's."

I rolled over and gave in, scratching her until she flopped onto her side with a satisfied grunt, legs twitching like she was chasing invisible squirrels.

It was impossible not to laugh.

She had that effect—turning grief into something you could actually sit with, breathe through, maybe even giggle at.

Rebecca sat up slowly, her morning stiffness ever-present now.

I could see the tremor in her hand as she reached for the cane beside the bed.

"Good morning, love," I said with tenderness underscoring my words.

She smiled through her usual Parkinson's brain fog.

"It's a better morning than most. The house smells like you're still alive, and Bella hasn't staged a mutiny yet."

"I thought about it," Bella muttered. "But I can't open the fridge without opposable thumbs. So, for now, I'm staying loyal."

I helped Rebecca to her feet, and we moved together toward the kitchen, slow and steady—like two aging ships heading to the same harbor.

Bella led the way, weaving expertly between our feet like a seasoned tour guide.

"You're walking better today," I said to Rebecca.

"It's either the meds kicking in," she replied, "or I'm simply so eager to have one of those delicious donuts you picked up last night at 'Glazed and Confused'."

"You and your sweet tooth." I laughed at her with an endearing smile.

While I got coffee brewing, Rebecca sat at the kitchen table until the coffee was finished. I poured her a cup of her favorite hazelnut, then she watched while I played sous-chef to those six glorious donuts warming in the microwave.

Bella sniffed. "Is that maple bacon I smell?"

She locked her eyes on those rotating bacon beauties like

BELLA

Tom Cruise dangling from a wire, looking for a landing spot. I swear if I had blinked, she would've rappelled off the fridge toward the microwave, snagging a maple-masterpiece sweet as she passed by.

"Wait your turn, Bella."

"Okay." With a dramatic sigh, she sat in front of the microwave with such poised dignity you would've thought she was attending an audience with a queen.

"Treat?" I asked, raising an eyebrow.

She nodded solemnly. "I'd say that I earned two for all of the extra emotional labor I provided in the past few days."

Shaking my head with amusement, I went to the pantry & got the bag of treats. I tossed her one, and she caught it mid-air with alarming grace. Willie Mays couldn't have done a better job! The second one? She sniffed, side-eyed it, and then flicked it across the floor like it was a hockey puck.

"This tastes like plywood. Uninspired. Were these even blessed?"

I nearly spit out my coffee.

After breakfast, Rebecca made her way slowly to the living room couch, and once she was settled, I decided to take Bella for a walk. Partly because she needed it, mostly because I needed it.

Being outside after chemo, breathing in something that wasn't hospital air or sanitizer, was like being granted parole.

Bella strutted down the sidewalk like a starlet on the red carpet at the Oscars.

Everyone knew her.

And now that she was talking—well, she became a one-dog neighborhood ambassador and self-proclaimed court jester.

"Morning, Mrs. Hanley," I called to our neighbor who was weeding in her flower bed.

Bella trotted up beside Mrs. Hanley's gate. "Nice hydrangeas. They are a bit overwatered, but I respect the effort."

Mrs. Hanley froze, blinked, and then looked around like she was being punked by a gardening show.

"Did your dog just compliment my yard?"

I smiled, shrugged. "She has strong opinions.

BELLA

"She's also writing a Yelp review for the squirrel that keeps pooping on our porch."

Mrs. Hanley's eyes widened. "She talks?"

"Only when she's not judging us silently," I said. "But yeah. It's new. We're adjusting."

Mrs. Hanley fanned her face with one hand. "Lord have mercy, I can't even get my husband to say two words before noon, and your dog's out here in my driveway giving speeches!"

Later after dinner, Rebecca and I sat close together on the couch, Bella sprawled across both our laps like a warm, opinionated blanket.

We didn't say much. We didn't have to.

"I like this," Rebecca said quietly, her fingers lightly combing through Bella's fur.

"What?"

"This peace. The three of us. Even if one of us is a little full of herself."

Bella yawned dramatically. "Jealousy is so unbecoming, Rebecca."

I reached over and kissed my wife's forehead. "We'll be okay."

She nodded. "I know. Somehow… I believe that again."

Bella opened one eye. "That's kind of my thing, you know. Hope. Belly rubs. And the occasional spiritual mic drop."

That night, as I lay in bed, Bella curled up by my side again.

Her breathing matched mine.

And just before I drifted off, I heard her whisper—

"You did good today, Michael."

"So did you, Bella," I whispered back.

There was a pause. Then:

"Tomorrow, I'd like to try that maple bacon donut if there are any left.

"I'm serious."

BELLA

And I laughed, right there in the dark, in the middle of all the mess and mystery and uncertainty.

I laughed because somehow, life—this broken, ridiculous, beautiful life—still had surprises left.

And one of them would soon be snoring softly by my side.

CHAPTER FIVE

The Talk I Didn't Know I Needed

It was late. The kind of night where time feels suspended — quiet, thick, sacred.

I sat at the edge of the bed, elbows on my knees, staring at nothing, rubbing my hands together like I was trying to warm the past. I was having one of my panic attacks.

Bella was beside me.

Close, but not touching.

She sat upright, calm, watching me like she'd been waiting for this night for years.

"You can feel it, can't you?" she said softly.

I looked at her. "Feel what?"

"That this moment's different. That something in you is ready."

BELLA

I exhaled slowly. "I don't know if I'm ready for anything, Bella."

"You are," she said. "You just don't believe it yet."

Her voice wasn't playful this time.

It wasn't sassy or sarcastic.

It was… knowing … illuminating. Like a candle lit in a dark chapel.

"You've been holding so much, for so long," she continued.

"And I've been waiting for the right night to say everything that needs to be said."

I didn't respond. I just kept staring at my aching hands.

So she began.

"Eleven years," she said. "We've been through eleven years together. That's almost one hundred in Chiweenie years!

"I've seen you strong. I've seen you sick. I've seen you screaming in silence, and laughing like your life depended on it.

"You survived three cancers. You held Rebecca up even when you were collapsing inside. You had to leave your job because of your health.

"You gave up things no one even noticed to keep this family from falling apart."

I felt the first tear slip loose before I could catch it. "I didn't have many choices, Bella." I said "My family comes first."

"I saw every time you cried in the closet or outside late at night," she said. "Every time you stared at the bills and wondered what else you could sell.

"Every time you worried if today was the day Rebecca wouldn't be able to get out of bed… and whether you'd be strong enough to lift her if she couldn't."

She stepped forward, placing her paw on my knee.

"You never let yourself be human," she whispered. "But Michael… you are.

"And you've done more than enough."

My voice cracked. "Then why does it still feel like I'm failing?"

"Because you care. Because you love.

"But love and guilt look alike in the dark. I'm here to remind you which one is which."

She paused, and then continued almost in a whisper.

"And Rebecca… she's extraordinary, you know."

"Yeah. I know."

"She's stronger than anyone gives her credit for.

"But she needs you, Michael.

"Not just for the pills and the lifting and the doctors.

"She needs *you*. Your attention. Your kindness.

"Your stupid little jokes that always make her laugh."

I smiled faintly.

"But she doesn't always need you to fix things.

"You try to do that too much.

"I know it's how you love—but sometimes, she just needs you to listen.

"To hold her hand.

"To let her be scared without rushing to calm her down.

"She needs your heart, not your solutions."

That one landed deep.

I looked down. "I guess I thought being strong meant having answers.

"No," Bella said. "Being strong means showing up, even when you don't feel strong.

"And letting someone else fall apart without trying to glue them back together in a hurry."

I nodded slowly.

BELLA

"Just love her," Bella said. "She already thinks you hung the moon.

"She loves you so deeply.

"You don't have to prove it every day. Just be there."

"I can do that," I whispered.

She climbed into my lap, paw-steps slow and tender. "Good. Because I won't be here forever."

I pulled back slightly. "What?"

She nodded, her eyes glowing in that eternal way dogs seem to look at us. "I'm getting tired. My hips ache. I sleep more. I'm almost fifteen-years old. I won't be around forever.

"But it's not today. Or tomorrow. But soon, Michael."

The room went still. My chest hollowed.

"I waited until now because you weren't ready before.

"You were just focused on surviving. But now? Now you're healing and I love watching it.

"You're now strong enough to carry Rebecca without falling yourself.

"That's why I can say all this. That's why I can talk at all. You needed me to help you get through the fire.

"Now, it's time for me to guide you to what comes next."

I touched her floppy ears, the tears returning.

"When the time comes—and it will—I want you to rescue another one."

I blinked. "Another dog?"

She nodded. "Someone scared. Someone overlooked.

"Someone like I was.

"No name.

"No wagging tail.

"Just waiting to be seen. And I want you to call him... or her, Puppy.

"That was my brother's name at the first home where I lived.

"He was the kindest, most gentle sibling imaginable."

BELLA

"You want me to replace you?"
"Never. I want you to continue what we started.
"Love's not something that runs out, Michael. It expands.
"You showed me that. Show it to someone else."
I swallowed. "I don't know if I can get another dog
"You will," she said. "And I'll be right there—watching.
"Nudging. Whispering, 'this one.'"

Just then our two cats, who made a living out of hiding strutted out of the closet and joined us on the bed. Winston and Penny. Blue-eyed, long-limbed, part-Siamese and all attitude.

MICHAEL J. WHELAN

They barely glanced at us as they leapt onto the windowsill with perfect grace – and zero regard for personal space.

Bella watched them fondly. "By the way, I've already told them everything."

I raised an eyebrow. "Told them what?"

She sighed. "That I talk. That I love them.

"That they're a bit dramatic, but still family."

Winston yawned loudly.

Penny jumped to the nightstand and knocked over the cup, then pretended she hadn't.

"They know about the plan," Bella continued. "They'll pretend not to care, of course.

"But when the new dog comes, they'll make space.

"That's what family does.

"Even if it means hiding under the bed for three days and hissing dramatically."

I smiled, even as my throat tightened.

A deep silence filled the room. Not empty. Full.

"I'm scared," I said, finally. "Of being alone."

"You won't be," Bella whispered. "I'll live in the fur you can't vacuum.

"The click of your steps down the hallway.

"The way Rebecca still laughs when she talks to herself and forgets I'm not in the room."

We stayed like that—an old man and his miracle—for a long time.

No more words.

Just the kind of stillness that heals instead of hurts.

Eventually, she broke the silence.

"Now," she said, nudging me, "let's head to the kitchen and get me one of those coconut ice cream bars from the freezer.

BELLA

"After you just ugly-cried all over me, I feel I deserve something special."

I let out a full, gasping laugh.

"You're the best therapist I've ever had," I said, standing up.

"Clearly," she replied.

"But I'm expensive. Tonight I charge two belly rubs and a promise that you won't give up."

"You've got it," I said. "All of it."

She paused at the doorway, her tail wagging slowly.

"You saved me, Michael. Now it's time to save someone else."

And just like that, she headed toward the kitchen—head high, paws light, tail dancing like it was writing her name in the air. I stood there in the hallway for a while, heart wide open.

And for the first time in years, I didn't feel terrified about tomorrow.

Because tonight, I'd been given a roadmap.

And a reason to keep walking.

CHAPTER SIX

The Best Day in a Long Time

It started with sunshine.
Not the dramatic kind—no golden beams slicing through the clouds like in a Spielberg movie.

Just a soft, unassuming light spilling through our kitchen window. The kind of light that doesn't demand anything.

It just arrives. Quiet. Gentle. Hopeful.

I was making coffee when Bella jogged in, tail swaying, face alert.

"Today's the day," she said.

I turned. "The day for what?"

She looked up at me like I'd just asked the most ridiculous question in the world.

"The day we stop surviving and start living again."

I squinted. "Are we still talking metaphorically? Or is this about you trying to sneak bacon off my plate?"

BELLA

"Both," she said. "But mostly the first one."

Rebecca came in a few minutes later, wrapped in her favorite cardigan, hair still wild from sleep. It was one of her better days. One of the days when she didn't need my assistance to get out of bed.

She leaned against the counter, her tremor subtle but there, like a metronome reminding us that time is always moving.

I kissed her cheek. "Morning, pumpkin."

"Morning," she said, eyeing the coffee.

Bella cocked her head, ears perked with curiosity.

"Hey Michael... can I ask you something?"

"Of course," I said, glancing down as she trotted beside me.

"Why do you call Rebecca, Pumpkin?

"She doesn't look very orange. Or round."

I laughed. "It's not about color or shape, Bella."

She waited, eyes wide, genuinely curious.

"The first autumn we spent together, Rebecca baked this ridiculous pumpkin pie from scratch.

"The crust was lopsided, and the filling was more 'soup' than 'slice.'

"But she was so proud of it.

"She wore this goofy apron with dancing pumpkins on it and had flour in her hair."

Rebecca laughed. "I loved that apron. I've still got it somewhere in the closet. The cats are probably using it as a blanket."

I smiled at my lovely wife, then continued, "And when I took a bite—well—it was awful. Just awful.

"But I told her it was the best pie I'd ever had."

Bella's tail wagged. "So you lied to her."

"I know. Lying's not right. But her eyes lit up with joy.

"So I ate the whole slice, then another."

Rebecca leaned in and hugged me.

"From that day on he's called me pumpkin, and the name just stuck."

"Every time I use the pet name, I remember that moment. Like it was yesterday.

"That silly apron. That laugh. That love."

Bella was quiet for a moment. Then she nudged my hand with her tiny nose. "That's the kind of love that makes dogs believe in humans."

I scratched behind her ears, smiling.

"And you, Bella, are the kind of dog that makes humans believe in second chances."

After a few moments of contented silence, Rebecca asked, "Do I get to be a part of whatever revolution Bella's planning for today?"

"She says it's the day we stop merely surviving and start living again."

Rebecca raised an eyebrow. "So… bacon?"

Bella gave us that toothy dog grin. "Now you get it."

We ate breakfast in the backyard. Something we hadn't done in far too long.

The sun was warm but not pushy.

The breeze smelled faintly of citrus and lavender from the bushes Rebecca had insisted we plant years ago.

For some reason Bella loved those plants.

Bella curled between us, her head resting on Rebecca's foot, her tail lightly tapping my ankle in rhythm with the wind chimes.

We didn't talk about cancer. Or Parkinson's. Or money.

We just… were.

At one point, I looked over at Rebecca, and for a second, she looked like she used to.

Not younger. Not stronger.

Just her. Alive!

The version of her that used to dance barefoot in the kitchen.

The one who whispered poems in my ear when we thought life was still stretching endlessly ahead of us.

And then she laughed—really laughed—at something Bella said about squirrels forming a union and demanding equal peanut butter rights.

I hadn't heard that sound in months. Maybe years.

Bella looked over at me and winked. "Told you. Today's the day."

We played a card game on the porch.

Rebecca beat me mercilessly and gloated like a seasoned gambler.

Bella chimed in with color commentary the entire time:

"Bold move, Michael. That's the kind of play that got us three types of cancer and a recall on your Juke."

By mid-afternoon, Rebecca was resting on the lounge chair with Bella curled up beside her like a warm comma between sentences.

I sat nearby, a notebook on my lap, scribbling nonsense.

Not because I had a story to finish, but because I wanted to remember the way this day felt.

The stillness.

The sun.

The way Rebecca's breathing matched Bella's.

Eventually, Bella sat up, jumped off the chair and walked over to me.

BELLA

"You know what today is?" she asked, a somber note in her voice.

"I thought it was Stop-Merely Surviving Day."

"It's also a gift," she said. "One of those rare days where nothing hurts, nobody's scared, and everyone's exactly where they belong."

I swallowed hard. "I want to remember it forever."

"You will," she said. "Because these are the days that make the rest of them bearable.

"The ones that remind you why you stayed."

I looked over at Rebecca. Her eyes were closed, a slight smile on her lips.

The sun had turned her face golden. Peaceful.

"She's going to need more of these," Bella said.

"I'll give her everyone I can," I whispered.

Bella laid her head in my lap. "I know you will.

"That's why I chose you."

That evening, we sat on the couch watching old movies.

Rebecca snuggled into my shoulder, and Bella stretched across both of our laps, looking for all the world like she'd won the lottery—and maybe she had.

She sighed deeply, content, then mumbled, "This is it."

"What is?"

"The best day we've had in a long time."

I looked down at her. "You think we'll have more like it?"

She smiled, eyes closing slowly. "We will if you keep showing up. You don't need big plans, Michael.

"Just presence."

And then, without opening her eyes, she added, "One day, you might even write a book about all of this.

"The love. The pain. The dog who talked too much."

MICHAEL J. WHELAN

I let out a quiet laugh, rubbing her ears. "You really think anyone would read it?"

She yawned. "They will if you tell the truth."

BELLA

And for once, I didn't overthink it. I didn't try to fix anything.
I didn't need to.
Because we were together.
Alive.
Still laughing.
And that was enough.

CHAPTER SEVEN

The Spotlight Finds Bella

We didn't plan the town hall event.

It started as a small invitation—Michael, the cancer survivor, local legend, cancer, Parkinson's, and Animal-Rescue advocate coming to share a few words about resilience at the community center.

Light refreshments. Folding chairs. Nothing dramatic.

And then, of course, Bella got wind of it.

"Oh, a live audience?" she asked, tail twitching. "Say no more. I'm in!"

"I'm just giving a short talk," I muttered. "Maybe fifteen minutes."

"You've survived stage-four cancer. Take care of your wife every day. Cried into your cereal, and still have a working sense of humor," Bella said. "Fifteen minutes is an insult.

"This is a revival."

BELLA

Rebecca chuckled from the kitchen. "You better put her name on the flyer, Michael or else you'll never hear the end."

"Featuring Bella the Talking Chiweenie. Spiritual Advisor. Life Coach. Squirrel Enthusiast," Bella announced like a Carnival barker.

"I'm going to need a headset mic and a bowl of cut strawberries and peanut butter treats in the green room."

I couldn't help but roll my eyes.

"It's a community center, not Carnegie Hall."

"Then they're about to level this night up," she said.

The night of the event, the room was packed.

Over a hundred people—some in wheelchairs, some with walkers, some clutching crumpled Kleenex and years of invisible weight.

They weren't here for a lecture. They were here for something real.

I started the talk with my story.

The diagnosis. The surgery. The fear. The ice cream bars.

The nights I thought I wouldn't make it, and the mornings I woke to realize that I had. At least for one more day.

As my talk was winding down, Bella trotted onto the stage, tail high.

There was a polite ripple of laughter—people probably assuming she was just there for comic relief.

But then she turned to the microphone, cleared her throat like a seasoned orator, and said. "Hi. I'm Bella."

Excitement and disbelief exploded in the room.

Gasps. Screams. A soda can clattered to the floor.

An older man in the front row crossed himself.

A teenager shrieked, "Dude, that dog just spoke."

BELLA

A woman clutched her chest, murmuring, "Of all the days to forget my blood pressure pills."

Half of the people thought it was a ventriloquist trick.

The other half thought it was the Rapture.

A little girl started crying. Her mother followed suit.

Phones were whipped out like pistols in an old western—recording, fumbling, and shaking.

Bella stood in the center of it all like a furry TED speaker. Calm as you please. Raising one little paw to wave at the crowd.

She waited. She let the hysteria settle into awe.

Then, with the poise of a preacher and the timing of a stand-up comic, she began, "For those of you who might not have heard, my name is Bella."

Again, there was a collective gasp loud enough to startle the janitor in the hallway.

Mouths dropped open. One woman dropped her purse.

Someone whispered, "Did that dog just talk again?"

And then came the laughter.

Then came the stillness.

When the room went hushed, Bella took over.

"I'm small.

"But I'm wise.

"Some say I'm adorable.

"I'm furry and shed a lot.

"And I'm here to tell you the truth. A truth you already know but that you keep forgetting."

She paused, letting the silence fall like a warm blanket.

"Love is messy. Life is loud. Death is rude.

"And still… here you are.

"Breathing. Showing up. Sitting in uncomfortable chairs in a room that smells like coffee and Lysol.

"That's faith. That tiny, stubborn spark in your heart that keeps whispering, that everything is going to be okay—even when your head is screaming otherwise."

Someone in the back started crying.

"I've watched people die.

"I've watched people fight.

"I've licked the tears of a man who wanted to give up and I told him, 'Not today, buddy.'

"I'm not here to fix you.

"I'm here to remind you that you're not broken.

"You're becoming."

You could hear a pin drop.

Bella sat down, softly, comfortably in the middle of the stage. She looked like a small puff ball.

Her voice dropped to a whisper.

"You don't need a plan.

"You need presence.

"You don't need answers.

"You don't need to be brave.

"You need arms wrapped around you."

Rebecca was crying now. So was the teenager in the second row.

So was the combat veteran with three medals and two missing limbs.

Bella looked over at me. "Tell them what I told you."

So, I did.

I told them about the night Bella imparted her wisdom to me in the kitchen while we ate ice cream.

The dream.

The breakdown.

The licking.

BELLA

The laughter.
The letting go of fear
After waiting to let my words resonate, Bella closed it.
"One more thing," she said. "If you're going through hell, don't stop. But don't run either.
"Walk slowly because I'm not as fast as I used to be.
"Do all of this with the people who love you most.
"And with a dog who thinks the world of you."

The standing ovation was instant and thunderous.
We rode home that night in silence.
Not the awkward kind.
The sacred kind.
In the backseat, Bella let out a sleepy sigh.
"I think I pulled a hamstring being that profound."

"You stole the show," I said.

"I didn't steal it," she murmured, eyes fluttering.

"It was always mine to begin with—truth is a powerful tool."

Rebecca looked over at me with tearful eyes and the softest smile.

"She's going to outlive us both, isn't she?"

"God, I hope so," I whispered.

And as we pulled into the driveway, under a sky too wide to understand, I realized something simple, beautiful, and true:

Bella wasn't just our *dog*.

She was our voice, our proof, our grace in motion.

And she had a few more chapters left in her.

CHAPTER EIGHT

What Bella Gave Rebecca

R ebecca was having a rough morning.
Her legs weren't cooperating.
Her balance off.

Her mood a little cloudy, like the Parkinson's had rolled in overnight with fog in its pockets.

I was about to hover—offer too many options, fix too many things—when Bella intercepted me with a pointed look.

"Give us a moment," she said.

"You sure?" I whispered.

"She's mine right now."

I stepped back and watched as Bella walked toward Rebecca, who had lowered herself into her reading chair with a wince and a sigh.

"Hey," Bella said, hopping up onto the ottoman. "Rough start?"

MICHAEL J. WHELAN

Rebecca nodded, rubbing her temples. "Yeah."

    They sat in silence for a while, the kind of silence women seem to understand better than men.

BELLA

I stayed in the kitchen, pretending to check the mail while eavesdropping through the thinnest wall of guilt.

Rebecca finally broke the silence. "I hate that he sees me like this."

Bella tilted her head. "He sees *you*.

"That's all. No judgment. Just love."

"But I used to be—"

"Rebecca," Bella said. "You still are."

Rebecca's eyes shimmered. "I'm so scared of being a burden."

"You're not a burden. You're the whole reason the weight is worth it."

That hit her. I saw her shoulders release.

Bella continued, her voice low, solemn. "You're allowed to mourn what you've lost.

"You're allowed to be mad, tired, and messy.

"But don't ever confuse needing help with being weak.

"There's a kind of grace in accepting love when it's offered freely.

"And Michael—he loves you with everything he's got."

"I know," Rebecca whispered. "But I miss being the one who takes care of him."

"You still do," Bella said. "He doesn't show it, but your strength is what keeps him going. And your laughter?

"That's his favorite sound in the world.

"And the way you love your animals…"

Rebecca smiled through her tears. "I don't laugh much these days."

Bella shifted closer, laid her chin on Rebecca's knee. "Then let's work on that."

And so Bella began telling a story—about the time she fell

off the porch chasing a squirrel she thought was chewing on our phone line.

About how she once faked a limp for three straight days just to get a second opinion from a younger, handsome vet.

Rebecca laughed—really laughed. The kind that shakes lose all the sadness in the corners of the heart.

Bella wagged her tail, proud and strong.

Then she got serious again.

"I need you to promise me something," Bella said.

"Anything."

"When I'm gone… let him grieve.

"But don't let him hide in it.

"Remind him of days like yesterday.

"The way the light felt. The smell of the lavender. The way you laughed during breakfast.

"He needs to remember that life isn't only what's taken. It's what's still here."

Rebecca nodded, her voice caught in her throat. "I will."

Bella licked her hand, slow and steady. "Good. Then I've done my job."

Later that night, after we'd put on music and danced slowly in the kitchen—Rebecca trembling, me supporting her, Bella watching us like a tiny chaperone—I asked her what Bella had said that morning.

Rebecca smiled. "She reminded me of who I am. And who you are."

"And who are we?" I asked.

She leaned into me. "People worth staying alive for."

And across the room, Bella curled up on her blanket, eyes closed, tail wagging once as if to say,

"Exactly."

CHAPTER NINE

Lavender and Light

The days passed quickly and we began to live our lives again.

We laughed and loved a lot more and worried a lot less.

And then it happened.

It was on a Tuesday. We were caught off guard.

No one ever expects it to be a Tuesday. Not the kind of day that sneaks up without drama or storm clouds.

Just soft light through half-closed blinds, toast cooling on a plate, and the sound of a dog sighing gently into the morning.

Bella hadn't eaten much the night before.

Just a few bites of grilled chicken from my hand.

She licked my fingers afterward, like it was a five-star meal.

Her tail wagged once, a slow sweep across the floor, and then she rested her head back on Rebecca's lap.

She had always been more than a dog.

She was a soul whisperer.

A therapist in fur.

A comedian with impeccable timing.

A fierce protector of hearts. And somehow, she knew.

"Michael," she said, her voice barely more than breath, "come sit with me."

I came. Of course I came.

Dropped the laundry. Dropped the act. Dropped to my knees alongside her.

I stroked her ears, memorized the lines on her face, the way her eyes still held that sparkle even as the light began to fade.

"I think it's time," she whispered.

"No," I said, as tears bloomed in my eyes. "Please, not yet."

"These tiny legs are so tired," she said, her breath hitching. "But what a journey we had, huh?"

Rebecca, who had been silent, reached down and touched Bella's back.

Her Parkinson's made movement harder now, but somehow her hand found its way to Bella's heart.

"You've been our everything," she whispered, and Bella closed her eyes as if to say, "I know."

"You gave me a name when I didn't have one," Bella said softly.

"You gave me love I didn't think I deserved.

"You saved me.

"And I tried—every single day—to save you back."

"You did," I said, voice cracking. "You still are."

"Promise me you'll take care of Pumpkin," Bella said.

BELLA

"And write all of this down.

"Someone out there is waiting for magic and doesn't even know it yet."

"I promise," I said.

"And… thanks for the fantastic belly rubs. They were top-tier."

Even now, she made us laugh through our tears.

That was her gift.

The levity in the heartbreak. The spark in the dark.

And then, as gently as a leaf falling from a branch,

A rose pedal falling off it's gorgeous stem, Bella let out one final breath—that felt like a whisper from the soul.

It sounded so peaceful. Not pained, not frightened, just ready.

And she was gone.

The room held its breath.

The world slowed, not with drama, but with reverence.

Shattered and crushed, I laid my head on her still body.

Rebecca reached over and whispered, "Run free, sweetheart. Run free!"

We stayed there. The three of us for what felt like forever. I didn't want to let her go. My body shook with tears and sadness.

Per Bella's wish, we buried her next to the lavender plants in the backyard, where she used to roll and sneeze and snort until she smelled like the most beautiful day in July.

In that place, the earth was soft, the sun respectful, and the breeze carried no judgment for the sobs that followed.

We marked the spot with smooth river stones. And silence. And a whole lot of love.

CHAPTER TEN

Honoring Bella's Request

Bella had crossed over the Rainbow Bridge. I felt the loss every day — not just in the memory of the way her body had stilled in my arms, but in the way the whole world seemed to exhale when she left.

One moment, she was there — warm, breathing, part of the air itself — and the next, the house, the sky, even the wind felt emptier, like a song missing its final note.

She was gone.

And yet… not.

The house afterward was unbearable.

The kind of quiet that didn't comfort — it accused.

The kind that wrapped itself around my throat in the middle of the night, squeezing until the grief poured out in broken, silent sobs.

Her food and water bowls stayed in the kitchen.

Her leash hung by the door.

Her blanket, still carrying the faint smell of her, lay in a heap she'd never straighten again.

Even Winston and Penny seemed lost, drifting from room to room, waiting for a sound that would never come.

What they would do to be chased by her one more time.

Rebecca, always the fighter, moved slower, spoke softer — as if raising her voice might shatter whatever fragile thing was keeping us upright.

I caught myself listening for her constantly — the jingle of her tags, the light tap of her paws, the little sighs she made as she curled up at my feet.

But there was only silence now.

And the silence was merciless.

At night, I'd sit at the edge of the bed, hands hanging useless between my knees, staring into the darkness where her little body used to be.

Sometimes I thought I heard her.

Sometimes I even called out.

But there was only the night, answering back with its heavy, aching stillness.

One evening, as the sky outside bled itself into purple and rose, Rebecca spoke the words that changed everything.

"We should go," she whispered, voice shaking. "We should honor her last request."

I lifted my head slowly, the weight of grief almost too much to bear.

"She wouldn't want the house this empty," Rebecca said.

Her hands were trembling.

"So much love… and no one left to give it to."

BELLA

I pressed my palms together until my knuckles cracked.

Somewhere inside, under all the wreckage, I remembered Bella's final message — the one I had felt, deep in my bones, the night she left:

"Love doesn't end, Michael. It only changes shape."

"Find another lost soul. Give them what you gave me."

I nodded.

And so we went.

The day we drove to the rescue center, it rained.

Not a violent storm — a soft, steady rain, like the earth itself was grieving, too.

I barely spoke on the drive over.

Every mile closer felt like a betrayal and a salvation at the same time.

My heart warred with itself — part of me aching to turn back, part of me desperate to feel something living in my arms again.

Rebecca's hand rested lightly on my thigh. A tether. A prayer.

"You're not replacing her," she said quietly. "You're carrying her forward."

The rescue center was small, hidden between two gnarled oak trees.

It smelled of damp straw, disinfectant, and a thousand restless hopes.

Inside, the noise hit us like a wave — barking, whimpering, claws scraping at metal cages.

I staggered under the weight of it.

So many souls.

So many abandoned hearts.

I wanted to run.

MICHAEL J. WHELAN

I wanted to fall to my knees.
And then...
A breeze.
Warm. Sweet. Familiar.
Lavender and sunshine and the softest, most impossible scent of home.
Bella.
She kept pushing me forward.
I turned to Rebecca.
She was crying, but she nodded, feeling it too.
Together, we moved through the rows of cages — past desperate faces, wagging tails, frightened eyes.

And at the very end, hidden in the shadows, we found him.

BELLA

A tiny, matted, disheveled Maltese, curled so tightly into the corner of his crate it looked like he was trying to disappear.

His fur was tangled and thin. His ribs threatened to poke through his skin.

But his eyes —oh, his eyes.

Wide. Haunted. Hopeful.

Exactly the way Bella's had looked all those years ago.

I knelt down, barely breathing.

The little dog inched forward, trembling, and pressed his tiny forehead against the cold metal bars.

I opened the crate without thinking.

And as I scooped him into my arms, the dam inside me broke.

Tears poured down my cheeks as I held him against my chest, feeling the desperate thump of his heart against mine.

It was then, cradling this broken, beautiful creature, that I heard Bella.

Not imagined. Not dreamed.

I heard her.

A voice as old as the stars, as soft as the first snowfall.

"Love doesn't protect you from pain, Michael.

"Love is the pain.

"It's the echo of everything beautiful you never wanted to let go.

"It's the price we pay for magic. Authentic love can be painful but it's always worth it.

"Would you trade it?

"Would you trade every moment — every kiss, every snuggle, every whispered goodnight — just to be spared this hurt?"

I sobbed into the little dog's fur, the kind of sobs that hollow you out and fill you up at the same time.

"No," I whispered. "Never."

Bella's voice wrapped around me again, like a warm, sacred blanket.

"It's magnificent, Michael.

"Warm like a sunbeam made just for me.

"And now... you have a new journey to begin.

"A new heart to heal."

I cradled the little Maltese tighter, feeling his heart stretch wider, ache deeper, and — impossibly — begin to heal.

I pressed my forehead against his and whispered, "What's your name, little one?"

Another warm breeze curled around us, and I smiled through my tears.

"Bella says your name is Puppy."

Rebecca reached over to stroke the trembling dog's ears, crying and laughing at the same time.

"Puppy," she repeated, her voice cracking with the weight of a hundred broken pieces beginning to stitch themselves back together.

After taking care of the adoption, we stepped outside.

The rain had stopped and the sky had broken wide open into color —lavender and gold, crimson and rose, weaving across the heavens.

And spanning it all, bold and breathtaking, was a perfect rainbow.

I held Puppy, pressed close against my chest and looked up into the sky.

And as I stood there, feeling the pain, the love, the gratitude too large for words, I sensed Bella's presence one last time: "You found me once.

"And now you've found him.

BELLA

"Love always finds a way home."

I closed my eyes, letting the tears fall freely, knowing finally, deeply, forever—that love is not the absence of pain.

Love is the reason you bear the pain at all.

Because some souls —like Bella's —never truly leave us.

Puppy adapted quickly. He even got along with the cats.

Every now and then he'd sit at the window, gaze out at the lavender, making the softest, most tender sound.

And as the evening wind stirred the trees and twilight wrapped the world in her quiet, Puppy perked his ears to a melody only he could hear. It wasn't a sound made by man or machine—it was the soul—song of the dog who came before him, drifting across the veil like a lullaby made of stardust and memory.

Like he knows she's still out there.

Like she's still teaching him how to love us.

And as expected, she's doing a fabulous job.

POSTSCRIPT: FROM BELLA

(With Love and Peanut Butter Breath)

Hi! It's me. Bella.

I know—it's quiet now. The bed feels too big.

The house creaks differently.

And the spot by the door where I always waited for you feels... hollow.

But I'm still here.

Not in the way I was. Not with paws. Not with breath.

But in the way that matters.

In spirit.

Michael and Rebecca… I need you to hear this.

I loved you more than anything in this world.

More than those Greenies and ice cream.

More than my naps.

More than that squeaky duck you pretended wasn't annoying.

You two saved me.

You didn't just rescue me from that shelter—you saved me from fading.

From being forgotten.

From going my whole life without knowing what real love felt like.

You looked at me—that scared, scrappy little mutt hiding in the corner—and somehow, you saw me.

Not my fear. Not my silence. Just me.

And you let me in.

BELLA

Into your home.

Into your heart. Into your most sacred spaces—your pain, your hope, your tears, your late-night ice cream cravings.

You gave me a life I didn't know dogs like me ever got to live.

And I gave you everything I had.

Every wag.

Every bark.

Every snuggle and sarcastic comment and face-licking rescue mission was me saying, over and over again.

Thank you. Thank you for giving me a name.

Thank you for trusting me with the pieces of your soul you thought were too broken to share.

When the days get heavy, and your knees ache, and your hands search for mine in the blankets—

I'll be there for you.

When Rebecca laughs, and it sounds like music—know that I'm dancing.

And when the coconut ice cream bar wrapper crinkles—that's me.

I'm just ahead now waiting for you.

My tail's wagging and the moment you show up—one day, far from now—I'll run to you like I never left.

Because I didn't.

Love Puppy like you loved me.

You'll always be my miracle.

And I'll always be your girl.

Love and Kisses Forever,
BELLA

Michael Whelan is a three-time cancer survivor and the former Director of Production for HBO Sports. He later became the Vice President and Executive Producer of productions at The Golf Channel helping build it from the ground up into one of the most innovative networks in sports television history. He spent decades producing legendary moments for millions of viewers—and wrote hundreds of documentaries until life handed him a far more personal and profound story to tell.

Michael is the full-time caregiver for his wife, Rebecca, who lives with advancing Parkinson's disease. He also advocates fiercely for cancer patients, mental health support, and the importance of compassionate care.

When illness and caregiving became the center of his world, Michael turned to writing as a way to survive—and to matter. His deeply honest, often humorous, and emotionally charged stories reflect the pain, perseverance, and beauty of the human experience. He writes for the underdogs, the exhausted, the caregivers, and the quietly courageous.

Today, millions follow Michael on Twitter/X for his authenticity, raw truth, and unwavering kindness to all. He doesn't sugarcoat the pain, but he never lets it overshadow the light.

At home in Orlando, Florida, he finds comfort and purpose with his wife, surrounded by their beloved rescue family: Bella and Bambi, their devoted dogs, and two wise, mischievous cats, Winston and Penny.

Every word he writes is an act of hope, a prayer for healing, and a reminder that even when life breaks your heart, there's still a story worth telling.

FOLLOW THE AUTHOR

X: @mikejwhelan
Facebook: @michaeljwhelanauthor

Printed in Dunstable, United Kingdom